D1685847

# KNOWING THE
## *Real*
# GOD

### DR. TELVA MILLER

XULON PRESS

I would like to acknowledge my photographer Jarrod Miller
and my Co-editor Dr. Laura Bonds

Xulon Press
2301 Lucien Way #415
Maitland, FL 32751
407.339.4217
www.xulonpress.com

Unless otherwise indicated, Scripture quotations taken from the King James Version
(KJV) – *public domain.*

Paperback ISBN-13: 978-1-66282-291-9
Hard Cover ISBN-13: 978-1-66282-292-6
Ebook ISBN-13: 978-1-66282-293-3

# Contributions

To my mother, Janice C. Knox, and my grandmother, Dorothy M. Pinellas. Thank you for all of your sacrifices, encouragement, and the love you have shown me. I miss and love you both so very much, but I know that I will see you again.

# KNOWING THE
## *Real*
# GOD

# TABLE OF CONTENTS

# Acknowledgements

*I give all the glory to my Lord and Savior. The inspiration for writing this book truly came from God. The Lord is my life and I can't do anything without Him. I pray this book will be used to inspire others to discover and live the life God has purposed.*

*To my husband, Mark Miller: Thank you for the years of support. You have always inspired me to take another step. I love and appreciate you immensely. May God continue to bless this union.*

*To my daddy, Albert Knox: Thank you for all that you did for my mom and each of us during our childhood years.*

*To my children, Shallondra, Jarrod, and Jelena: There were times I called you for financial assistance or just a word of encouragement and you were there to support me. Thank you, I love you.*

*To my daddy, Earl Holmes: Thank you for your support during my storms.*

*To Marilyn Miller: Thank you so much for always being there for Mark and I.*

*Charlotte, thank you for always being available. Thank you for your inspiration and encouragement when I wanted to give up. I appreciate and love you immensely.*

*Dr. Bonds, you and I have grown through our doctoral studies and personal challenges. Thank you for being my co-editor, friend, and mentor. I truly love and appreciate you.*

*To my sister Paula: Thank you for being there while I was going through my storms. I love you.*

*Melissa, thank you for the wonderful care you provided for my mother. I will always be grateful.*

# Introduction

$I$ believe that each of us develop our individual experiences with God. I am certain that we are all destined for a purpose assigned by God. It is the development of a personal relationship between you and God that creates a conduit for one to discover his/her earthly purpose. One must cultivate a relationship with God by offering your time, resources, prayer life, flexibility with direction, and the ability to deny self. In Luke 9:23, it states that "If anyone would come after me, he must deny himself and take up his cross daily and follow me." This scripture simply states that Jesus was saying one needs to put to death personal plans and desires, turning your lifes over to Him and doing His will daily.

# CHAPTER
## *One*

# MY BEGINNING

$\mathcal{A}$fter graduating from high school and moving on to college, I poured my efforts into my educational journey. I made a conscious decision to be successful in spite of the mistakes I made during my middle and high school years. Research has shown that father involvement between the age of seven and sixteen years could safeguard children from psychological challenges later in their adult lives, especially for females. I have subsequently learned the catalyst to many of my poor decisions regarding relationships, prior to my marriage, stemmed from not receiving acknowledgment and acceptance from one of my biological parents. This pivotal missing link resulted in the acceptance of sub-par relationships, such as physical abuse or being the other woman in a relationship. I realize without equivocation that God covered my mind.

I remember a college professor saying to me, *"Hodge, you will never make it."* The tears poured like a flood. I could not fathom how an educator could utter such harsh words to a student. Those words subliminally shattered my confidence and shouted failure. After several years of college,

I became pregnant. I did not allow the pregnancy to stop my progress and I had the full support of my parents. After giving birth to my daughter; however, I failed out of nursing school. My mother travelled to Tallahassee to help me gather my things and I returned home. Once again feeling like a failure, I had some very important decisions to make. Although I was a new mom, I returned to school and the rest was history.

My personal journey of knowing God began approximately fourteen years ago. I have always felt a special calling over my life. I was raised in the church, graduated from Valencia Community College in 1990, but felt as if something was missing. There were moments in my college journey that I would call on God and He always made His presence known to me. I remember praying to God about a husband and asking for specific requirements; and thankfully they all manifested in the one who I chose to marry in 1993. In 1995, we purchased our first home and I accepted a full-time position as a nursing instructor. I had always possessed a strong passion to teach and help others. After approximately six years of teaching nursing students, I acquired a passion to help nursing students pass the state examination. I researched and applied to an organization that was looking for instructors. I submitted my resume, only to be told that I did not have the required teaching experience. I was absolutely devastated!!! I called my grandmother and shared with her the feedback that I received, and she uttered the words, *"Do your own program."* Those words ignited a fire on the inside and the catalyst for something new.

In 2001, I began to research the intricacies of starting a business. I researched areas that included obtaining a business license, developing a business plan, opening a business account, and securing an accountant. I also reached out to the Florida Board of Nursing (FBON) to determine the requirements for starting a program to assist graduate nurses in passing the National Council Licensure Examination (NCLEX) state examination and, lastly, collected curriculum materials needed for the course. Finally, approximately four months later, Millers Nursing Review was birthed; I knew that God's hand was over this program. I advertised for my first class and received ten newly graduate nursing students. The first class was an absolute success and I truly felt like this was my calling.

I vividly remember three hurricanes that swept through Kissimmee, Florida in 2004. My family and I woke up to the roof shingles hitting the ground. Once the final hurricane swept through, my home was uninhabitable. We had just enough time to grab our insurance documents, my purse, and the clothes on our backs. This began my journey of knowing God on a deeper level. I began to watch and listen to different ministers on the television, listen to CDs, and take many notes. I became intrigued about gaining more knowledge about God. I learned more about God's Word and the essence of how His Word should be used. Over the next couple of weeks, my roof collapsed, and everything in my home was destroyed. My husband and kids moved in with my parents simply because we had no place to go.

Approximately six months later, we were blessed to find a two- bedroom apartment. Although we were transitioning from a four- bedroom home to a one-bedroom at my parents' home, we signed a one year lease to provide us with our own place to live. As I continued to pray, I could see the hand of God. The insurance money that we received from the home paid to rebuild our home, paid for the apartment rental, and all the essentials needed for survival. I remember learning the Scripture that stated to "call those things that be not as though they were" (Rom. 4:17). Rehearsing this Scripture literally empowered me to walk through my home, which displayed mold, fetid walls, collapsed ceilings, and flooded floors and cite God's Word according to Romans 4:17. I began to order CD's and books to align my thoughts with God's Word from authors, such as Joyce Meyer, Creflo Dollar, and T.D. Jakes. I progressed from saying and reading God's Word superficially to saying and believing it whole- heartedly. My faith escalated to another level; I began to thirst for more of His Word day and night.

Approximately one year later (2006), our home had been rebuilt completely; it was as if we moved into a new home. We were so excited. Within the first year of being home, I clearly heard the Holy Spirit say it was time to move. I remember pondering the thought of how to tell my husband that after all the hard work he put into our home that it was no longer for us but for someone else. I developed a routine of waking up between three and six a.m. to seek God. I joined a church pastored by a couple who were clearly called by God to deliver the Word. I was so intrigued with their style of teaching and preaching. I tithed and, attended Wednesday night Bible study and church every Sunday. My husband did not support the ministry and felt as if the organization was strictly money-driven. Despite my husband's belief, I stayed faithful to the ministry. I learned to recognize God's voice through a thought, an idea, a Scripture that I read, or simply hearing the Word of God.

In 2006, the Holy Spirit laid on my heart to start a remedial program. This course is required by the Florida Board of Nursing for those who were unsuccessful after three attempts of taking the nursing examination. I remember saying to God that "I do not want to remediate." I later reached out to the board to see what the requirements were for initiating the program. The person who provided me with the information asked me if I belonged to a school. My response was *"I am a private business,"* and she laughed at me and stated that I probably would not be approved. My response was thank you for the information and I requested the necessary documents. One essential requirement for approval was an affiliation agreement with a hospital. I reached out to the educator at Osceola Regional Hospital. I made multiple attempts, but no one would return my call. I woke up the next morning and called out sick from my full-time teaching job to travel to the hospital to visit the educator.

That morning, I woke up at approximately 4:30 am. I walked directly to my closet to pick out an outfit and then proceeded to complete my personal time with God. I sat down to pray, and the Holy Spirit said, *"Go and pick out a suit."* I was the only person awake in my home and I exclaimed, *"A suit?"* I got up from the table to return to my closet and I selected a blue suit. I returned to the table to complete my personal time with God.

A few hours later, I went to the hospital to contact an old colleague to assist me with finding the educator. I explained to her my endeavors and my unsuccessful attempts at reaching the educator. She stated to me, *"Let's pray."* After prayer, she called the chief nursing officer (CNO) and explained my situation, asking if she had a few moments to meet with us. The CNO stated to come to her office in forty-five minutes. After the meeting, she agreed to an affiliation between the hospital and me. God validated that I heard His voice and that is why He said to wear a suit. Approximately five months later, I became the first business to achieve Florida Board of Nursing Remediation approval in the tri-county area.

I remember being in church doing praise and worship and feeling as if God was telling me it was now time to trust Him for a business location.

I had only been renting locations prior to feeling that prompting for the business. I would rent conference rooms and ultimately college classrooms. The prompting grew stronger and stronger. I finally said to my husband, *"God is telling me to step out and believe Him for a location."* I immediately started to think, "How are we going to be able to afford a location?" I reached out to my personal friend and adopted sister by the name of Tashema Rembert, who was a realtor and loan officer. After I shared the vision, she immediately agreed to assist me.

My husband and I were out driving one day, and God showed me a vision. The vision was me standing on the stage of my current church teaching. I was mesmerized!!!! The miracle envisioned was the church purchasing a new location and that current location becoming vacant. I reached out to Tashema regarding that vision, and she immediately contacted the company who owned the location. I was astonished with the feedback regarding the monthly rental for this storefront location. The monthly payment was starting at approximately $5000.00 per month and would increase by a certain percentage annually. Fear immediately set in; I began to second-guess my hearing from God. I remember praying more and reminding God of His Word. I would quote God's Word by saying, *"My God has not given me the spirit of fear"* (2 Tim. 1:7) and *"I can do all things thru Christ who strengthens me"* (Phil. 4:13). I had to meditate on God's Word daily to overcome the fear that I had succumbed to. After a couple of months, my mountain-top faith had returned. I decided to trust God at His Word and move forward. I completed the application process and God did it again. The application was approved and Miller's Nursing Review had a new home. My faith was growing exponentially, as God continued to validate that I was hearing His voice. God met the financial obligations; the resources poured in like a flood for approximately two to three years.

# Chapter
## *Two*

# Hearing and Moving in Faith

*I*n 2007, my grandmother died. I remember when the church read the resolutions (a formal declaration of the relationship between the deceased and their church); I realized that I did not receive one from my church. I was devastated. My husband's words resonated in my ear and I suddenly realized that it was time for me to leave that particular church. I respectfully submitted a letter explaining that I would no longer attend the church. Feeling frustrated and lost, I was uncertain of where my new fellowship home would be. I remembered my grandmother uttering these words prior to her dying: *"Please give my pastor a chance."* She further stated that she was a very genuine and loving person. I gradually returned to my old church to hear and see this pastor by the name of WillieBell Coleman.

I attended this church every Sunday. Her spirit, demonstration of love to others, and personal demeanor exemplified the walk of Jesus. Her love extended to the poor and to those who had a six-figure income. There was absolutely no difference or favoritism shown. I spent a total of ten years following this amazing woman of God.

In 2010, I started to see a decrease with the business finances. Things became more difficult; there were increments when there was not enough income to pay the rent. I found myself having to call the company to explain the financial hardship, as well as to make payment arrangements. There was a season when the business phone had been disconnected. I remember the utility company entering the building and stating, "*We are here to disconnect your utility services unless you can pay within the next ten minutes.*" I began to second-guess my hearing God's voice. I remember pondering why God would allow this to happen. I was angry, hurt, disappointed, and in total disbelief about the current situation. I can recall my husband saying, "*Where is God now?*" To add insult to injury, we were behind with our mortgage and had to apply for a modification to prevent foreclosure on our home. My husband and I were facing a few goliaths.

The winding path had me in a place of despair. I honestly wanted to quit. I did not realize that while on the journey with God, you will experience some very challenging positions, but one should always remember that even Jesus was tempted. Individuals must believe that when your faith is challenged through temptation, do not relinquish your beliefs about God. Rehearse this:

No temptation has seized you except what is common to man. God is faithful; he will not let you be tempted beyond what you can bear. But when you are tempted, he will also provide a way out so that you can stand up under it (I Corinthians 10:13).

Deuteronomy 8:2 states that, "You shall remember that the Lord your God has led you in the wilderness these forty years that He might humble you and testing you, to know what was in your heart." Embracing your valley experiences teaches you to humble yourself before God, as well as to recognize that you cannot do it without Him. I cried out to God asking for help. I verbally expressed how I could not do this alone. God always prevailed and made a way when I did not see a way.

After a few months of many valley experiences and seeking God, the Holy Spirit said to me, *"RN to BSN."* My immediate thought was **What?** I had absolutely no desire to start a college. I wrote down what I heard and continued with my normal routine until it was validated by God. Random nursing students would say things such as: *"Have you ever thought about starting a nursing program?"* Or *"You would really do well with starting a nursing program."* I knew that God was challenging and calling me to something bigger. In addition to the aforementioned, I began the Doctoral program. I had to consciously accept the challenge of starting a new chapter in my personal and professional career.

I began the research for starting a nursing program. After several months of researching the Florida Board of Nursing statutes and other nursing programs, I initiated the process. Habakkuk 2:2-3 states, "Write the vision down and make it plain on tables, that he may run who reads it" James 2:14 states, "Faith without works is dead." I worked diligently to balance my time between preparing nursing students to pass the nursing state exam, creating the curriculum for the nursing program, and working on a doctoral degree. I spent many hours behind closed doors secretly preparing. My children would say things such as, *"You don't have a life."* My form of relaxation was simply just watching a movie or eating out occasionally. I realized that my personal enjoyment had to succumb to the mission.

As I continued to work faithfully on getting the nursing program approved, I reached out to a family member who was a grant writer. She agreed to drive from Jacksonville for a face-to-face meeting. After a two-to three-hour meeting, she respectively requested some time to read the documents before making a decision. After approximately two weeks, I received a phone call. Rakinyna (grant writer) agreed to write the grant. My first question to her was how much would she charge. Her immediate response was, "*I will not charge you unless the grant receives approval.*" I was elated!!! Her response further validated that I heard from God. Months of research and hard work went into preparing a $4,000,000.00 grant. The grant included salaries for teachers and supporting staff, purchase of a school location, and equipment. The day finally came for submission of the grant for approval. We prayed diligently. My faith truly believed that God was going to approve this grant.

Approximately three to four months later, I received a call indicating the grant was not approved. I experienced a myriad of mixed emotions, ranging from anger to sadness. My faith level declined to a valley level. I simply could not fathom why God would not allow the grant to be approved. In anger and haste, I took all of the work that had been completed for the college and shoved it into the file cabinet. In anger, I yelled out to God, "*When You show me the money, then I will move forward with opening a college.*" The documents sat in the file cabinet for months. I continued with teaching the NCLEX Review and Remedial course.

As time continued to pass, it was time to begin another review course. I continued with the same process. On the second day of a new course, there was a young lady from the class who respectfully asked to speak with me in private. As she approached my desk, she pulled out an index card. She stated that she was a pastor who had never passed her nursing examination. She further stated that after the first class day, God spoke to her on my behalf. On the index card were things that she felt that God had spoken. The first few words that she uttered were *"God said that you were to start a school and that you got frustrated because something did not work out and you quit."* She also stated that, *"He wants you to continue moving and to trust Him to work it out."* The tears began to stream!!!! I never uttered one word to anyone in the class regarding my efforts of starting a nursing program. That information had to come from God. God was speaking through her about my incomplete assignment. The conversation truly convicted me; this was the catalyst that reignited me to get restarted. During the next couple of weeks, I continued with moving forward with getting the approval of the nursing program. I submitted the application, catalog, fees ($1,000), and all supporting documents to the Florida Board of Nursing for approval. Correspondence was received a few months later requesting suggested changes. Once the corrections were made and the documents were resubmitted, it was now time to attend the board meeting for approval.

Once the board meeting started, shortly thereafter, Millers College of Nursing was called to the podium. I was experiencing tachycardia (fast heart rate), trepidation, and sweaty palms. After meeting some opposition from a couple of the board members, it was time to vote. The vote was 50/50 or a tie. The chair voted for the program and the approval status was received. God's presence prevailed. My husband and I were ecstatic. The time had now come to receive approval from the Department of Education (DOE). God blessed me with the most supportive program representative. She was compassionate, supportive, hard-working, and, yes, a Christian. We worked tirelessly to get the program ready for approval. I received donated equipment from the local hospital and a school that was going out of business. The final drawback was the remaining $3,000.00 needed to submit the application. We had saved a total of $1,000.00. A former student walked into the college and stated, *"God told me to bless you."* She handed me an envelope. I opened the envelope, and there was a $3,000.00 financial gift. This completed the $4000.00 needed to submit the application. Ephesians 3:20 states that, "God will do exceedingly and abundantly above all that we can ask or think according to the power that works within us."

Finally, it was time to begin the nursing program. The first class consisted of ten nursing students and started in 2011. I would like to add that my husband has always been supportive in every area of my personal and professional journey. I believe that when one immerses into his or her God-given assignment, the support of the significant other is imperative.

As we transitioned into 2012, it was now time to hire more staff and continue to trust God to meet the budget. Currently my staff included my husband, my daughter (secretary), and myself. I remember when I was looking for an admissions director. We advertised and received quite a number of interested applicants. After careful review, I narrowed it down to two applicants. My secretary called and scheduled the interviews. After interviewing both applicants, I prayed and asked the Holy Spirit who I should select. I remember hearing, *"Hire them both."* I immediately thought, *Our budget cannot cover both.* Although both had the same title, they were skilled in different areas. I strategically created a schedule where they were both working only two days per week. They both accepted the position. Approximately one month later, one of the admissions director accepted a full-time position with another school. God showed me that what she brought to the table was unfamiliar to the other admissions director. Proverbs 3: 5-6 states to "Trust in the Lord with all your heart and lean not on your own understanding; in all your ways acknowledge Him and He shall direct your paths." God is so amazing when you trust Him. The years of 2012 and 2013 continued to provide me with multiple opportunities to trust God.

The first group of nursing students included ten students. I was so excited to be used by God on this level. I remember God prompting me to pray for one of the students. The next day I called her into my office and told her that I was led to pray for her. I further explained how I was instructed that she was having difficulty with getting pregnant. Once I uttered those words, she began to cry and explained her struggle. She and her husband had been trying for approximately ten years. We simply held hands and I called on God. I reminded my heavenly Father of His spoken Word. Approximately two months later, God showed me in a dream she was pregnant. The next day I arrived to work a little earlier than normal. Shortly after my arrival, this particular student arrived. As she proceeded to walk into the door, I greeted her and further shared my dream of her being pregnant. She looked at me in total disbelief. She went to put her books down and returned to where I was sitting. She confessed that she had just completed a pregnancy test and she was pregnant. She had not shared this with anyone because she simply wanted to make sure everything would be ok. I stated, *"This blessing is from God and you can tell the world because everything is going to be fine."* She has since graduated from the program and has a lovely son. She and her family refer to me as being their angel. I can't express enough how faithful God is when you release your trust to Him.

The year of 2013 catapulted me into a season of challenges. There were many times we were unable to pay the rent. I reached out to the leasing company a number of times, explaining the financial hardships. Periodically we would receive eviction notices. I fell into a pit of despair; however, I was determined not to leave prior to honoring the timeframe outlined in the lease.

As we neared the end of the lease, our realtor found multiple locations to view. One of the locations was approximately twenty miles from our current location. My administrative team and I went to see the location. We loved it!!!! I felt as if this was Millers College of Nursing's new location. I learned early in my Christian walk to always pray before making big and small decisions. Proverbs 3:5-6 states: "Trust in the Lord with all then heart; and lean not unto thine own understanding. In all of thy ways acknowledge Him, and He shall direct thy paths." James 1:5 states: "If any of you lack wisdom, let him ask of God." I felt as if I was making the right decision to purchase this location; however, I needed confirmation from God. While I waited for confirmation from God, we decided to move forward with a contract. James 2:17 states: "Faith without works is dead." There should always be a corresponding action as a believer.

After receiving the final contract, we quickly noticed the final monthly payment had increased by $400.00. The significant increase was the confirmation that I needed to walk away from the deal. We decided to continue looking at the other locations selected by the realtor. The next facility was smaller, but it encompassed two joint locations with different owners. I learned later this location had been previously a nursing program. My husband and I decided to move forward with leasing the two locations. My realtor contacted both owners and the negotiating started. We needed approximately $20,000 to move into the new locations. God supplied every dime that we needed through the hands of old and new students. Roughly three weeks later, we received both signed leases. One ultimate concern was additional funding, as I now had to increase my staff to support the number of new students coming into the program. After receiving a couple of bank declines, my parents decided to assist financially by borrowing equity from their home. My mother truly wanted to assist me with the success of the college. I later received $35,000 from the equity loan. God continued to confirm I was walking in the right direction.

I later discussed with Tashema (realtor) my concerns with leaving the old location without paying the outstanding fees. She later scheduled an appointment with the leasing company. On the day of the meeting, I sat down and explained that my company was no longer at that facility, but I wanted to initiate some form of a payment arrangement regarding outstanding fees. The manager pulled the file and stated the outstanding balance owed was approximately $90,000. I was utterly astounded. I simply asked, "*What form of a payment arrangement can we set up?*" His response was, "*I appreciate your honesty and desire to pay the debt.*" He further stated that many tenants move out during the night and they never heard from them. "*I will reach out to you to see how the debt can be settled.*" I gave him my personal cell number. After a couple of months, I called on several occasions. The manager never returned my call. My realtor and I came to the conclusion the company must have cancelled the outstanding debt. We never heard from the company after the meeting. God was covering me and working it out the entire time.

Several months into the new location, we quickly discovered this was a new level. Larger giants were appearing. The monthly budget increased to $30,000. A couple of the nursing groups were not paying their tuition on time. God wanted me to utterly depend on Him and not on the students. The monthly payroll averaged $10,000. The home equity loan provided by my parents truly assisted with increasing expenses. During the year of 2014, I graduated with my doctoral degree in education, and I continued to hear more from God regarding sowing into the lives of others.

In January 2015, God prompted me to give my personal friend Charlotte $4,000. She resided in a different state and was attending college. Once God had spoken to me about giving her the monetary gift, I prayed and waited for confirmation. I reached out to her and I shared what God had spoken. She simply cried and stated her need for the gift. God was teaching and speaking to me about obedience as well as showing me how I was a vessel. Later in January, the Holy Spirit prompted me to give my aunt $5,000 to assist with funeral expenses from the loss of her daughter.

On February 7, 2015, I was prompted to give my very dear friend Laura $2,500.00. On February 12, 2015, I moved forward with the financial blessing. God was meeting my needs as I continued to sow into the lives of others. On March 3, 2015, the Holy Spirit prompted me to sow $7.000.00 into a particular ministry. I remember gasping for my breath and verbally saying, *"Lord is this you?"* I ultimately moved forward with giving into that particular ministry. On March 6, 2015, I went to my director of admissions home to pick up her granddaughter. There was a prompting to give her mother $500.00; I did not give it to her on that exact day. I spoke to my admissions administrator later in the week about my prompting. She immediately called her mother and placed her on the speaker. She asked her mother *"Are you believing God to meet a personal need?"* Her mother stated that she needed $467.00 for her car payment. I wrote the check out in the amount of $500.00. I had to continue to spend time with God daily because the amount and frequency of seeds continued to grow, and I needed to move as God instructed and not be in fear. I continued to sow the seeds as prompted and bigger blessings continued to manifest. Payroll continued to be met, and Millers College of Nursing was able to shoot and run our very first television commercial. My staff and I were so excited.

During the month of September, giants were appearing from many directions. We experienced financial deficits with payroll, payroll taxes, funds needed to hire a tax attorney, the mortgage, and the decrease of student scores for the nursing program. The low pass rate could have ultimately placed the nursing program in jeopardy. I continued with my personal time with God. I truly believed that if I fainted or abated the process, I would fail in every area. I remember in the month of November, one day before payroll, I needed $15,000. My finance manager, who was also my son-in-law, went to check the mail. There was a flyer from American Express with a pre-approval offer of $60,000. He and I took the necessary steps for approval, and Millers received $44,000. God exceeded my expectation. The next morning, I checked the business account and the funds had been directly deposited. Payroll was met and my faith continued to grow. I cannot express the importance of believing in God and His awesome power.

# CHAPTER
## *Three*

# DADDY ISSUES

$\mathcal{I}$ was the oldest of five siblings. I was raised by my mother and my grandmother. Three of my siblings had a different father. My mother got married when I was about eight years of age. My stepfather played a key role in my life and truly was a blessing to each of us. As for my biological father, my mom told me that his name was Alfonza Hodge; however, my aunts and uncles told me that my father's name was Earl Holmes. I did not care for either one because I felt abandoned by both men. The literature reveals that a father's absence leaves an indelible mark on a daughter's mind, soul, and spirit, as she blossoms into adulthood.

As I matured through middle and high school, I chose only to acknowledge my stepfather, as he was the only father figure in my life. Experts have cited that:

Adolescents who experienced father absence had lower self-esteem, engaged in sexual activity at an earlier age and had lower general achievements compared to adolescents of intact dyadic families. Furthermore, a negative impact on personal relationships was noted. (East, Jackson, & O'Brien, 2006, p.289)

Imagine growing up not knowing who your biological father is and not receiving any form of acknowledgment. I never received a birthday card, a graduation gift, a lunch date, or a phone call. I poured all of my efforts into my mother and grandmother, but secretly harbored bitterness and resentment through my entire adult life.

I remember attending church and seeing the man who I was told by my family was my biological father. He would enter into the church with his wife and not a glimpse in my direction. My thoughts were how on earth could he walk past me without acknowledging my presence. Anger would resonate at the sight of his presence. I was told by various sources that he did have other children. I can say wholeheartedly that I became apathetic and abrasive at his sight. My vortex of emotions remained un-waivered until he left the church. There was never any verbal contact between Earl Holmes and myself. I did have minimal contact with Alfonza Hodge (the other possible dad). In 2012, he passed away from a heart attack. I did attend the funeral; however, I did not shed one single tear.

In November of 2015, I received a call from my cousin. She very subtly asked if I believed that Earl Holmes was my dad? My response to her was, *"All of our family members have said that he is, but my mother has continued to deny the possibility of Mr. Holmes being my father."* My cousin then asked me if I would be open to going out to a job site where her husband and Mr. Holmes were working together. My initial response was *"Absolutely not."* She spent the next few minutes of our conversation trying to convince me of why I should go. After repeatedly saying no, she uttered some very earth-shattering words. She stated, *"I would give anything to be able to talk with my dad."* Those words pierced my soul, and I agreed to go and meet this man who walked past me for years.

Once we reached the work site and walked inside, I found myself face to face with my alleged father. He looked at me and uttered the words, *"Come and give your papa a hug."* For just a moment, I was able to dismiss my negative emotions and embrace him with a hug. I was completely at a loss for words. My cousin stated, *"You guys need to talk."* She further stated that I should tell him my birthday and age. I could not believe that I finally had an opportunity to share my thoughts, yet uncertain of what to say. He asked me how I was doing. I responded respectfully and accordingly. I shared my birthday and age. I discussed my husband, my children, and my grandchildren. I shared my birth name and many of my successful accolades. I needed him to know that I was not a failure. The experience of our initial conversation was genuinely like meeting a stranger. After spending a little time talking with him, we exchanged numbers. I must admit that I was uncertain of how to process the myriad of my overwhelming emotions. I was suddenly face to face with someone that I consciously chose to leave in my past. On my way home, I remember thinking, "Oh wow, God, now what?"

The next morning after my Bible time, I was sitting at the table grading papers. My phone rang and it was a call from my dad. I said to my husband, who was sitting next to me at the time, *"I guess he was thinking of me."* I answered the phone and I said, *"Good morning, Mr. Holmes."* From that day forward was the beginning of something new. I would love to say that every day was magical; however, this relationship required a lot of work. My dad and I spoke daily. The relationship then evolved into him and me spending time with each other. My husband was reserved only because he did not want me to be hurt. My dad and I planned lunch dates at least one to two days per month. The conversation of DNA testing finally crept up into one of our in-depth conversations. I politely asked him if we could complete the DNA testing. His response was, *"Sure, if that is what you want."* I immediately started searching for a location and the price. Once I gathered all of the details, I contacted him with the date and the cost and he moved forward with making the payment.

The test date was scheduled for the day after Thanksgiving in 2015. We met at the designated location, completed the test, and then went on a lunch date. On the day after the DNA testing, I sat at the table to do my daily Bible time. I was very anxious about the results simply because I had developed very strong feelings and the possibility of him not being my biological father was daunting. I remember thinking what if he is not my father. The emotional bond for Mr. Holmes created trepidation and uncertainty. God knew what was in my heart. As I continued to study the Word on this particular day, my eyes fell upon the scripture: *"Your hope will not be disappointed"* (Prov. 23:17). I simply cried. Those were the most comforting words that I could have read on that day. I felt as if God was saying to me it's ok. As the weeks continued to pass, we simply continued with our daily phone conversations and daddy-daughter dates. Spending time together provided an opportunity for us to learn each other's temperament. I must admit that I had multiple struggles. I would constantly hear from others that my sister was the apple of his eye. He would consistently say that *"I love all of my children the same."* My response was *"How is that possible and you just met me?"* His response never changed. The other struggle was learning that he raised other children. I could not conceive his denial of me and acceptance of others. His response was unwavering and that was,

*"Your mom told me that you were not my daughter."* I confirmed his response with my mother and she validated his response. The rehearsal of my denial created a constant, unspeakable fury. I would continually reach out to God, asking for help. My emotions were on a perpetual roller coaster.

On December 5, 2015, the DNA results revealed that Mr. Earl Holmes was my biological father. He and I were both elated. I could only give God the glory for orchestrating all of the events and piecing this puzzle of my life together. My mother was absolutely stunned. Her immediate response was, *"I am so sorry; I would never intentionally keep you away from your dad."* It was now time to meet the rest of the family. I knew my dad's wife; however, I did not know any of my siblings. I did not anticipate the resistance that I faced from members on his side of the family. There were times when I would say to him, *"I am being rejected by your loved ones and because it is so painful, I need to step away for a while, but I will stay in touch."* It was difficult for me to comprehend the negativity and rejection. I continued to pray because I needed every ounce of God's strength not to walk away. I would rehearse to myself that God did not unveil the truth about my biological father only for me to buckle at the knees because my feelings were hurt.

Day after day, I continued to pray for strength. I remember telling my dad that I will never visit his home. As a prayer warrior, I simply could not comprehend how to acquiesce under the negativity. After several weeks, I finally made my first visit to his home. I was feeling extreme trepidation, as I did not know how my presence would be accepted. Once I arrived, to my surprise, I was welcomed with open arms by my dad and his wife. I slowly began to warm up to the rest of the family. Time slowly crept by, as I spent time getting to know my new family. God was teaching me that it does not matter who dislikes you; *"just stay mindful that you were sent by Me."*

Month after month continued to pass, and each visit became a little easier. I learned to love my siblings. I wanted the family to know that I did not come to take anything; I simply wanted to be accepted and acknowledged by my father. Dad slowly started to introduce me to other family members outside of his home. I started to feel as if I truly was a part of the family. If I could echo one message, that message would mimic Proverbs 3:5-6: "Trust in the LORD with all your heart and lean not on your own understanding; in all your ways submit to him, and he will make your paths straight." The love continued to grow stronger for my dad, and the relationship blossomed.

I would love to say that I never experienced feelings of being left out or personal thoughts of not being a priority in his life, or that he did more for my siblings, but the truth is I did and continue to occasionally have those thoughts. I have also learned of so many other people my dad has assisted. The enemy continued to remind me on every level that he loved others more than he loved me. I would have to counter those thoughts with biblical Scriptures such as 2 Corinthians 10:5, which states, "Cast down arguments and every high thing that exalts itself against the knowledge of God, bringing every thought into captivity." This simply means replace your thoughts with the Word of God. To accept the negative thoughts implies that God made a mistake and that He is not purposeful. I trusted God, and I knew that meeting my family was not a mistake.

It has been five years since I met my father. He has since experienced the loss of many family members, had surgery, and yes occasional daddy/ daughter disagreements. My intent was to be there for him on every level. It truly has taken God's strength to forgive, love, and move forward. One very important tradition that he and I have formed is our daddy/ daughter dates. Once a month, he and I meet at a pre-selected restaurant; this is our designated time to chat and chew. This is also a time for us to put all the cards on the table. He and I openly express any unresolved issues or simply reflect on our relationship and the positive bond that has evolved. Although there have been times when anger has emerged, the love that has grown always triumph any negative situation. I could have never reached this type of peace without inviting God into this relationship.

The message that I would like to leave is forgiveness must triumph. I would also like to express that forgiveness is impossible without God. We are human beings and subjected to positive and negative emotions. Feelings were not created to be the captain of your decisions. The Scripture reminds us that, "As a man thinks in his heart so is he" (Prov. 23:7). The direction of your emotions (positive or negative) can take you into a very dark or happy place, and the mind is the battleground where the fight originates. Stay strong, prayerful, and positive, and simply allow God to work through you so that you can bless others while they are going through their struggles.

# Chapter
## *Four*

# God Allows the Storms

*I* heard a pastor say that there is always something God does in your history that becomes the substratum to your destiny. Even when you are in a dark season, the only thing that has failed was the thing you had in your mind. God does allow the suffering so that we can see and experience Him on a deeper level. I had attended several mandatory Florida Board of Nursing meetings regarding my nursing program; the issues were derived from the low-test scores. I felt as if all of my hard work with assisting the graduates to pass the state exam was not working. I continued with my worship and found myself asking God, *"Do I continue?"* I would listen to sermons that included messages such as nothing you have gone through will be wasted; or rise to the height of your calling; or just because something is not working in your life does not mean you are under satanic attack. I heard a sermon and the pastor stated, *"When the thorns and thistles rise up, it is time to move into another dimension"* Genesis *3:18.* There will be times on your journey when it seems like your skills are being wasted.

The year of 2016 ushered in many valley and mountain-top experiences. The Word and various sermons helped me to keep my momentum. I vividly remember a pastor saying, *"Your next will be connected to your now and to try it again even after multiple failures."* The NCLEX scores continued to escalate after implementing the various strategies the Holy Spirit showed me. I continued my assignment regarding the college and other areas of my life, although everything appeared dark. I attended my final board meeting in 2017. I came to the realization that the time-frame allocated to increase the program scores was here, and I had not reached the benchmark. I had two choices: one was to voluntarily close the school, or, two, allow the Board of Nursing to close it. I voluntarily decided to surrender the school. That was a very tough decision, especially because I knew without equivocation that God instructed me to open it. I realized at this point God was doing something new in my life. I remember silently thinking to myself *Where do I go from here?*

During the next stage of this journey, the money and staff (with the exception of Gleny, my administrative assistant) were gone. I could feel the Holy Spirit directing me to finish what I had started. I had approximately fourteen students left. The mixture of students included a day program and an evening program. I taught both classes, and quite often no money was left to pay me a salary and personal bills continued to mount up. I must admit this was very hard. I would work as if I was working for hundreds of students. I would also go to the hospital so that my students could complete the clinical component of the program. I remember running into two of my old faculty members who were currently working for another school. The encounter left me numb. They both asked me, *"How and what are you doing?"* I openly expressed that I was completing a teach-out and that I voluntarily surrendered the college. I also remember acknowledging how painful the journey had been, but that I knew that God was not going to leave me in this place. Imagine for just a moment the students who you assisted were established in their careers and making more money than you. I found myself thinking about the story of Joseph and how God allowed him to be thrown in a pit. I would also think about Job and how prosperous he was, and yet all was taken from him. The Bible states that God is not a respecter of persons (Acts 10:34) and if He turned things around for them, then one day He would do the same for me. I continued my daily devotion and, every day, maintained a spirit of expectancy from God. I would love to tell you that this was the end of my anguish; however, the journey continued into the next chapter. I truly found myself crying out to God and begging Him to regulate my mind.

# CHAPTER
## *Five*

# MY JOB EXPERIENCES

*I*n January of 2017, my mother was diagnosed with right lung cancer. I watched my mother consistently lose weight prior to the diagnosis, and all of her doctors correlated the weight loss to stress. My world was shattered; however, I believed God for a healing. I remained at her side with her various appointments. I needed my mom to know that I would be there for her no matter what. My step dad, Albert Knox my sister, and I tag-teamed to ensure she was taken care of. We would assist with her baths, getting food, and giving her medications. My auntie Paula and Wendell were also amazing with assisting my mom. My husband was my rock. He was always there to do whatever needed to be done.

I continuously stayed in contact with my mother's oncologist to ensure that proper care was rendered. I remember when she was admitted to the hospital to get a lung biopsy for a definitive diagnosis. I experienced a myriad of emotions, such as fear, faith, and uncertainty. My grandmother Dorothy Pinellas, who was also like a mom to me, passed away with cancer in 2009. The pain was incomprehensible. The thought of revisiting emotions of grief was unbearable, regardless of my strong faith. I was now faced with making a decision to close my college, my finances had dwindled, my remediation course was rescinded by the Florida Board of Nursing, and now my mother was sick. I felt as if God had abandoned me. The college resources had dwindled; I had to downsize and could no longer pay any staff members or for the two suites. The owner of the second suite came and served us with an eviction notice because of the inability to pay the rent. I cried out to God and continued to pray, even when it did not seem like it was working. I truly felt like Job during this time. I would state the Scripture, Job 13:15: *"Thou He slay me yet I will trust him."*

Once the diagnosis was confirmed, we decided to move forward with radiation. Although she was extremely frail, I knew she could handle the process. She experienced approximately two weeks of intensive radiation treatment. My mother being the strong woman she was would be able to cope with receiving this very aggressive treatment needed to save her life. After the treatment was completed, she was able to breathe better and, for a moment, to function at approximately 50 percent capacity. She was very tired; however, that was the expectation after receiving the radiation treatment. The favorable progress was noted for approximately one month. The pain to her right side of the chest reoccurred, and she did not feel comfortable in a lying position. She simply wanted to sleep while sitting. I became more aggressive with my efforts of reaching out to her oncologist about the next phase of treatment. Additional tests were ordered, and finally the physician decided to move forward with admission into the hospital to initiate chemotherapy.

The day we were all waiting for finally arrived. I met my dad (Albert) at the hospital to assist with the admission process. My mom was placed in a room and, within hours, many unforeseeable medical mishaps began to occur. Once she was settled in bed, the nurse completed taking her vital signs. My mother's blood pressure was extremely elevated. Within approximately an hour or so, she had to be transferred to the step-down intensive care and then ultimately to the intensive care unit (ICU). Her blood pressure was not responding to the medication, and she was exemplifying an irregular heart rhythm. The nurses worked quickly to start an IV line, complete an EKG, and draw bloodwork to check her electrolytes (lab values). The nursing staff made the ultimate mistake of asking her to lay back, and that triggered a very anxious and combative demeanor. Please keep in mind that I did not disclose to any of the medical staff that I was a registered nurse. My mom was so anxious and now her oxygen saturation (o2 sats) dropped from the mid 90s to low 80s, and she was not responding to the oxygen that was given. Finally, medication had to be given for relaxation. After the above steps were taken, we were asked to go to the waiting room. After approximately an hour and a half, we were notified regarding the various measures that had to be taken to stabilize her. I left the hospital that particular night thanking God for not experiencing any of those medical setbacks while she was in the home. I am always looking for God in the trenches and for opportunities to thank Him while He is working.

As the days turned into weeks, I would leave work and stop by the hospital to visit my mom. The medical staff had 24-hour access to me in the event I was needed. It appeared from the surface she was getting better. I remember stopping by one day and she said to me the doctor told her she needed to be placed on hospice. I was livid. My response to her was, "*I don't care what the doctor thinks. He is not God and we are believing for a healing.*"

I remember one day that I stopped by to visit and one of my graduates was her assigned nurse. I was so very happy because I knew she would was in good hands. She was assisted out of bed to the chair. I truly believed God was going to heal my mother.

On April 28, 2017, I received a phone call from Melissa (graduate from Millers College) encouraging me to stop by the hospital. I remember driving to the hospital and sitting in the parking lot. I felt impending doom as if I knew something was about to happen. I could not get out of the car. I called my daughter, and she came and sat in the parking lot with me. I finally decided to drive home. I got up early the next morning and decided to go and visit my mom. Upon my arrival, she was asleep. Family members and friends stopped by throughout the course of the day, but we could not get her to wake up. As the day progressed, a chaplain stopped by to offer prayer. Finally, after about eight to ten hours at the hospital, I decided to drive home. I told my dad if she wakes up to please give me a call. Within an hour of being home, he called and told me, *"You are not going to believe this but your mom is awake."* He further explained the nurse who took care of her when she was initially admitted kissed her on the forehead and she woke up. I thought wow!!!! That is so typical of my mom because she was always flirtatious. I slept very well that particular night. The next day, Sunday April 30th, I decided not to go to church. This was very unusual, as I was very faithful with my church attendance. My day began as usual, which was prayer, personal time with God, shower, and the continuation of my routine for the day. I arrived at the hospital and one of my sisters was at my mom's bedside, holding her hand. I could see her labored breathing and she appeared very anxious. I sat next to her and asked her, *"What's wrong?"* I further stated to her that I was going to have the nurse bring her some medication to help her relax, and then later try and remove the BiPAP machine to give her face a break. She is typically excited for the temporary removal of the BiPAP machine, but not this time. She aggressively shook her head no.

I walked out of the room to speak with the nurse. I explained my concerns and requested medication to assist her with relaxing. Once the medication was given, I sat at my mom's bedside until she fell asleep. I never dreamed that would be the last time I would see my mother alive. After approximately twenty minutes, I stated to my dad that I was going home and to call me when she is awake. I walked to my car and headed home. On my way, I said the most heartfelt, selfless prayer any child could speak. I prayed, "*God, let Your will be done. I do not want my mom to suffer.*" Once I arrived home, approximately thirty minutes later, my dad called and stated, "*You better come now.*" My husband and I immediately rushed to the car and headed back to the hospital. While driving at an extremely fast pace, we saw my sister driving as well. I looked over at my sister Paula and I saw her crying. My phone rang approximately one minute later, and it was my dad. He stated, "*She is gone.*" My heart stopped; the pain was unimaginable. I could not believe my mom was gone. Once I arrived at the hospital, I threw myself across her body and cried. I checked her pulse and there was nothing there. My world was shattered. I could not understand after praying and believing for a healing why God would take my mom. Many of my family members gathered at the hospital.

I stayed with my family members until the funeral home staff arrived with the gurney to take her body. I found myself experiencing extreme anxiety and fear, as I did not have the strength to watch them remove my mom's body. The experience seemed so surreal. I ran to the elevator, continued to my car, and I simply cried. I could not take any more pain. I remember taking medication that night simply to help me sleep and to temporarily suspend the pain. I honestly do not remember if I prayed and spent time with God the next day. It appeared that I was walking in a never-ending nightmare.

The following day, I went to my dad's house, as it was now time to assist with making funeral arrangements. My dad asked my husband to take the lead with making the funeral arrangements. The next six days seemed as if they were eternity. My husband contacted the funeral home and truly assisted with making essential decisions. My sister Paula and I went shopping to find her a dress and other essentials that were needed. I continued to pray and cry out to God for my strength. My best friend and roommate from college came to assist me through this very difficult time. Finally, May 6th, 2017 arrived. This was the day of her funeral. The pain was truly unbearable. I gave my mother her final kiss. As the services continued, I looked up and saw the ICU nurse who took care of her. He had previously lost his mom a year prior to cancer. The church was completely filled, as we celebrated the homegoing service for my mother. The following day was Mother's Day, and I could not muster up the strength to attend church. Two days after burying my mother, I returned to work. That was such a difficult transition. I could hear my mother saying, "*I am gone. Go back to work and finish what you have started.*" The process was so very difficult, but I prayed so hard for strength. I literally had to teach on some of the same topics that I watched my mother deal with. There were times when I had to excuse myself from the classroom because I could not hold back the tears.

I continued to pray for strength. I believe that as a Christian and believer, there is no part of our lives where God should be left out. I prayed for direction, healing, regulation of my mind, body, strength, and for others. I found myself saying to God, *"Thank you Lord for allowing my mom to live seventy years because there are many who lost their moms at much younger ages."* My prayer and personal time with God intensified because the pain was so intense. As the weeks turned into months and into years, I could feel God's presence in my life. The tears were not as regular, my mind was a little stronger, and my teaching became a little easier. I continued to thank God for His grace and mercy. I would love to end this chapter by telling you the money was returned, I was no longer experiencing foreclosure, and God gave me a new school: however, none of those things occurred. I swallowed my pride and reached out to various people who I had helped in the past. I stayed on this trajectory for approximately three years after the passing of my mother.

I remember walking down the stairs one day to look for a bill on the counter. I silently pondered, *"God, when are You going to turn this situation around?"* As I sifted through the mail, I found a letter from my IRA company. I opened this account approximately ten years prior and had not contributed any money since the time of opening. I actually had forgotten that I had it. There was a prompting from God to open the letter. During this time, Mark and I had *no money*. I opened the letter, and there was approximately $9,000 in the account. I was mind blown and began to see more and more how God was directing my steps. I truly felt like a child being cradled in the arms of my heavenly Father.

In January of 2020, I had an appointment to visit my gynecologist for my annual visit. The doctor who walked into the room was someone who

I had not seen previously. She proceeded with my pap smear and breast examination. Once she completed her examination, she expressed her concerns about what she had felt in my breast and my cervix. She further explained that she would provide me a prescription to have a mammogram and a cervical ultrasound. My anxiety level escalated exponentially. To further add to my anxiety, I was waiting on the approval of my health insurance. This simply meant that all expenses had to be paid out of pocket. I remember calling my dad and explaining the situation and asking for financial assistance. After carefully listening, he replied, *"How much do you need?"* I gave him an estimated figure and he simply stated, *"No problem. When do you want to come by and pick it up?"* I responded in a childlike manner and said, *"Thank you, Daddy."*

The next day, I called to set up an appointment to have the mammogram done. Unfortunately, they were completely booked for the next two months. This was extremely unorthodox, as I had been coming to the same company for years and never experienced such a long delay with setting up an appointment. The receptionist further stated that if I needed an appointment sooner, there was an office in Orlando with availabilities as soon as a few days. I proceeded to secure the appointment.

Finally, the scheduled day arrived to have the mammogram. I proceeded to check in. While waiting, I noticed this young lady who walked in while talking on her cell phone. She signed in and was later called to the back. Approximately ten minutes later, I was called to the back. After putting on the gown and waiting to be called into the room, I see the young lady who I had previously seen in the lobby. I said hello and the conversation continued. She expressed her anxiety because historically after her mammograms, she always had to follow-up with an ultrasound because of the history of problems with her breast. After listening to her concerns, I asked her if I could pray for her and she immediately replied, *"Yes please."* Right after the prayer, I was called into the room to complete my procedure. I later walked out and she was still waiting to be seen. I gave her my phone number to call once the ultrasound was completed. I received a call from her approximately thirty to forty-five minutes later. She was simply elated the ultrasound report was negative. We both began to thank God. I later realized how God re-routed me to that facility to simply pray for someone who needed prayer at that time. God knows what we need and how to use each of us to be a blessing to others.

My routine, which included spending time with God daily, continued. The Scripture states, "God will not leave thee nor forsake thee and that He is not a man that He shall lie (Heb. 13:5; Num. 23:19). God is not a microwave type of God. Metaphorically speaking, He operates like the conventional oven. You will not race across the finish line, but simply pace yourself for the journey.

# CHAPTER Six

# My Year of Breakthrough

The year of 2020 has introduced a new level of giants for all. This year has ushered the nation into a pandemic. As a nation, we were faced with an unprecedented disease process, where many lives have been lost. The COVID-19 virus has completely created life as never seen before. "The COVID-19 virus spreads primarily through droplets of saliva or discharge from the nose when an infected person coughs or sneezes" (World Health Organization, 2020). The virus has claimed the lives of so many. The potency of the virus led to the shutdown of our country. Many businesses were closed, people lost their jobs, mental health issues were at an all-time high, crime rates were elevated, and people were confined to their homes outside of work or to pick up groceries.

I am a conventional, face-to-face teacher. I am suddenly faced with a government order like so many others of not leaving my home. I was experiencing extreme trepidation, as I was uncertain about how to navigate through this new way of living. My oldest daughter, who is also an educator, stated to me that I needed to learn how to teach online. She further stated that she and her husband would assist me with learning the process. I stepped out on faith and advertised my first online class. I had to find God in this new place. Suddenly, I began to receive graduates who were ready to take the course. I was elated; this was another level. God showed up in this new place and sustained me with revenue during the pandemic. I continued the same process for months, and God continued to meet me in this new place.

Approximately nine months into the year, a couple of students reached out to me for assistance. Their nursing program was experiencing issues with low NCLEX scores and halted students moving forward with graduation. I simply replied that I was only completing a teach-out process and no longer accepting new students. This particular student was relentless. She would not give up and would call me daily, expecting a different response. I finally stated, *"Let me pray and see if this is God."* Her response to me was, *"Ok, Dr. Miller."* Approximately two-three days later, I woke up early and as I began to get up, the Holy Spirit spoke in my spirit and reminded me that I stated to Him, *"God, help people to see the glory of You in my life."* I later discovered this student had been praying to God, asking for help. I spoke with her later that day. I suddenly received approximately twenty more students from the same school. My revenue increased by an additional $12,000.00 per month. I was truly flabbergasted at what God had done. Ephesians 3:20 states that, *"God will do exceeding and abundantly above all that we would ask or think according to the power that works within you."* I knew there was a shifting that was occurring in my life.

I shared this wonderful news with my husband, my prayer partner and very close friend, Charlotte, my children, some of my family members, and my previous pastor, who I now refer to as my second mother,

Pastor Smith. I wanted all to know the amazing work God was doing in my life. I felt in my spirit God was not done. I had a spirit of expectancy and truly believed the next step was a job as a dean of a nursing program. I stepped out on faith and bought a new suit for my anticipated interview. Approximately two months later, I received a call regarding a position as a dean for a nursing program. I literally forgot that I had submitted the application. Approximately one week later, I interviewed for the position. A student told me two months earlier that God told her in the spirit that someone was looking for me. She also prophesied that I should look for a big window and a burgundy bookshelf unit. After the interview, the owner stated, *"I would like to show you your office."* The office had a big window and the burgundy bookshelf. To my God be the glory!!!!!

# CONCLUSION

*a*s I bring this part of the book to a close, I would like to say my journey is not complete. I have settled into my new position as the dean of a college. I am currently completing the teach-out with Millers College of Nursing and moving forward with the remedial program. My allegiance is to my Lord and Savior. On my daily route to the new job, or if it is a day that I am sitting at home, I continue to invite God into it all. I am simply nothing without God. We are living in a world simply filled with hate, in which so many people are being killed daily. Mathew 24:12 simply states, "And because iniquity shall abound, the love of many shall wax cold." The world needs Jesus. We must recognize we are absolutely nothing without Him.

I need my husband, children, and those who are in and around me to know and see through me how real God truly is. I purposely walk past people known and unknown, and greet them with a smile or simply just a humble "hello" because I am mindful of those who may be dealing with sickness in their bodies, need their minds regulated, are homeless, or struggling with the loss of a loved one. God has allowed me to experience loss on so many levels. As a result, He has taken me to a new level. The world cannot see the pain that I have endured, yet they see the success I have achieved. Know that through it all, God covered me and it would not have been possible without Him. Therefore, consider Jesus's journey: He endured the suffering of the cross so that we might have a second, third, or as many opportunities needed. God is so faithful!!!! We must trust Him in the good and in the bad. I will not give up until I have attained everything He has purposed for me.

I would like to encourage anyone who has read this book to join me on this Jesus journey of helping others. Hebrews 13:16 states: "Do not neglect to do good and to share what you have, for such sacrifices are pleasing to God." Galatians 6:2 states: "Bear one another's burdens, and so fulfill the law of Christ." Philippians 2:4: "Let each of you look not only to his own interests, but also to the interests of others."

I pray that my transparency in this book will inspire and uplift individuals to seek God and His righteousness first: then, with patience, they will discover their dreams, goals, and the manifestation of God's blessings in abundance. I would like to reiterate it may not happen according to your time, but I can absolutely assure you if you wait, you will not be disappointed.

# BIBLIOGRAPHY

East, L., Jackson, D. J., O'Brien, L,O. (2006). Father absence and adolescent development: a review of the literature. Journal of child health, 10 (4), 283-295. DOI 10.1177/136749350606869

# About the Author

Dr. Telva Miller is a nursing educator and currently is the dean for Riggs College of Allied Health and CEO of Miller's Nursing Review. I enjoy sharing and spreading the Word of God to others. I pray this book will be an inspiration to others in their personal journey with God and if so please email me at telvamiller@aol.com

CPSIA information can be obtained
at www.ICGtesting.com
Printed in the USA
LVHW100741010821
694140LV00004B/38